Plant Traps

Pauline Cartwright

Contents

Plants	2
Plants with Traps	6
Big and Little Traps	14
Plant Traps	16

Plants

Look at this plant.

It has a flower.
It has a stem.
It has leaves.

flower

stem

leaves

The flower has food for insects.

Some plants don't have food for insects. The insects are food for the plant!

Let's take a look.

Plants with Traps

Look here. This plant has leaves.

leaves

The leaves are insect traps.

Insects come to the plant.
They stick to the leaves.
The insects are food for the plant.

The leaves of this plant are insect traps.

An insect comes to the trap.
It sticks to the leaves.
The insect is food for the plant.

The leaves of this plant are insect traps.

Insects look in the trap.
They fall in!
The insects are food
for the plant.

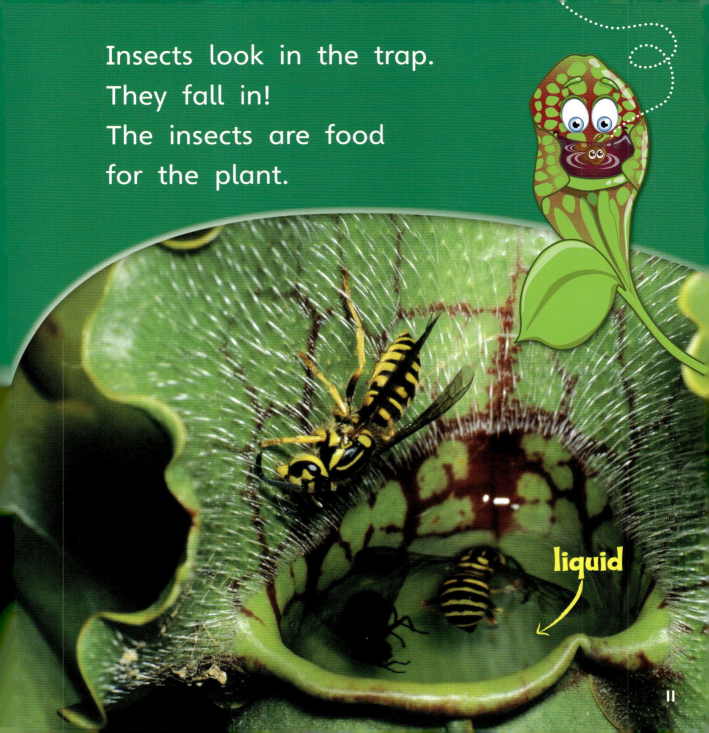

liquid

These leaves are insect traps too.

An insect comes into the trap.
The trap snaps shut!
The insect is food for the plant.

Big and Little Traps

Some plants have little traps.
They can trap very little things, like insects.

But look at this plant.
It has a big trap.
It can trap a frog!

Plant Traps

Plant	Leaves
	sticky
	sticky
	liquid
	trap
	liquid